...and gone forever

By the same author
DECLINE OF STEAM
STEAM FINALE NORTH
STEAM RAILWAYS IN INDUSTRY (with Horace Gamble)
EACH A GLIMPSE ...

First published 1994

Reprinted December 1994
Reprinted July 1995

A catalogue record for this book is available from the
British Library.

ISBN 0 86093 526 4

Oxford Publishing Co. is an imprint of Haynes Publishing,
Sparkford, Nr Yeovil, Somerset BA22 7JJ

Designed by Colin T. Gifford
Typeset in Rockwell Light
Printed in Great Britain by Butler & Tanner Ltd, Frome and
London

Colin T Gifford

...and gone forever

OPC

Oxford Publishing Co.

Thanks to:
Paul Gifford, for taking these pictures.
Louise Gifford, for typing the manuscript.
Kiry Gifford, for her forbearance.
David Percival, for general consultation.
Ian Young, for constructive interest.
Derek Lawrence, for always saying 'yes'.
Peter Nicholson (editor), for
patience and understanding.
And my publisher, for allowing me to
'do it my way'.

Preamble

Whilst compiling this book, I came to realize that it is not only the steam locomotive that has disappeared from everyday life but also the way of life itself. It may well be that affection for these scenes is derived as much by evocations of the period as it is from the steam train and its environment. I remember the open front door, the bobby on the beat and back streets where children played; a time when a football team could be readily identified by the colours of its strip, or the make of a car by its shape. These were the days of soap-box carts, scooters, Saturday morning pictures and holidays by train. I was fortunate to record this particular era and hope that these photographs convey the 'feel' of the times. The steam locomotive epitomises those days but it, along with most of what I have recorded, is now a memory encapsulated for me by the distant sound of a whistle floating on the still night air. Steam was here and gone for ever...

5. The waiting room window on the up platform at Whitwell, Derbyshire, 26th September 1964.
6. Stalker Castle and Loch Linnhe from Appin, 17th June 1963. 7. Rush-hour at Clapham junction 6th April 1965.

8. 35011 *General Steam Navigation* in Clapham Cutting with a Waterloo – Bournemouth train, 14th September 1964. 9. 34053 *Sir Keith Park* overtakes a Shepperton local as it approaches Earlsfield with a Weymouth train, 26th October 1964.

10. 34006 *Bude* and 34082 *615 Squadron* on Bournemouth line trains at Waterloo, 4th February 1962. 11. 40030 with empty stock and 44658 light at St Pancras, 5th June 1958.

12. 60145 *Saint Mungo* and 60021 *Wild Swan* with evening departures at King's Cross, 10th May 1963. 13. 75031 at Broad Street with a train for Tring, 31st May 1962. 14. 1024 *County of Pembroke* at Paddington with a Weston-super-Mare train, 24th July 1958.

15. 42134 leaves Marylebone with a High Wycombe local train, 20th August 1960. 16. 42102 with a train for Tring leaves Euston, 2nd March 1960. 17. 61622 *Alnwick Castle* passes 69724, the station pilot, as it leaves Liverpool Street for Felixstowe, 18th July 1957.

15

16

18. 61630 *Tottenham Hotspur* on the turntable at Liverpool Street, 18th July 1957. 19. 72008 *Clan Macleod* on the turntable at Stirling, 5th September 1961. 20. 61289, 45659 *Drake*, 44814, 92086 and 46100 *Royal Scot* at Derby motive power depot, 25th June 1961.

21

22

23

24

21. 31615 being turned at Redhill, 4th October 1962.
22. 31816 leaves Guildford with a train for Redhill,
2nd January 1965. 23. 31857 with a Redhill train, leaves
Betchworth, 5th October 1963. 24. 31816 crosses the
Basingstoke Canal as it leaves Ash for Reading,
2nd January 1965.

25

26

25. 44680 crosses the Shropshire Union Canal at
Mollington with a train for Birkenhead, 5th March 1967.
26. L94, with a spoil train, passes over the Grand Union
Canal between Watford and Rickmansworth,
18th November 1969. 27. 48602 runs beside the
Rochdale Canal at Castleton with a southbound freight,
23rd August 1967.

28. 61337 and 44841 about to cross the Rochdale Canal near
Walsden with the Newcastle – Manchester stock train,
18th June 1964. 29. 70026 *Polar Star* and 43075 with the same
train at Eastwood, 5th September 1964.

30. 73134 and 73069 head one of many special trains, run towards
the end of steam on British Railways, over Saddleworth Viaduct,
20th April 1968. 31. 44694 and 44662 leave Bradford Exchange with
trains for Bridlington and Skegness respectively, 26th August 1967.

32. 44968 and 44972 take water at Crianlarich Upper with a Fort
William – Glasgow train, 20th July 1961. 33. 47668 (left) and 47377
shunt, Shaw Street yards, St Helens, 7th June 1966.

34

34. 1368 and 1367 on Weymouth Quay,
10th September 1961. 35. Victoria dock,
Aberdeen, 12th June 1962. 36.
60837crosses the King Edward Bridge,
Newcastle with a southbound oil train,
30th September 1961.

35

37. *Roker,* a R. Stephenson & Hawthorns 0-4-0CT, works beneath the shipbuilding gantries at Doxford, Sunderland, 24th September 1969.
38. A Merchant Navy class 4-6-2 approaches St Denys with a Bournemouth – York train, 11th February 1967. 39. No. 26 *Whitwell* leaves Cowes for Ryde, 7th August 1965.

40. A Class O2 0-4-4T near Cement Mills Halt
with a train for Cowes, 16th October 1965.
41. No. 20 *Shanklin* starts away from Wroxall with
a Ryde Pier Head – Ventnor train, 11th September
1965. 42. No. 14 *Fishbourne* leaves Newport for
Cowes, 17th October 1965. 43. A Class O2
leaves Mill Hill with a Cowes – Ryde train,
16th October 1965.

44. 6840 *Hazeley Grange* passes through Snow Hill, Birmingham with a northbound freight, 6th February 1965. 45. 47289 shunts coal wagons at Williamsthorpe Colliery, 12th September 1967. 46. 65873 heads coal empties north of West Hartlepool, 27th September 1965. 47. No. 58, a R. Stephenson & Hawthorns 0-6-0ST, shunts wagons on the north side of Corby Iron & Steel Works, 14th November 1965.

44

45

48. 41835 in the Devonshire Works of the Staveley
Iron & Chemical Co. Ltd, 19th April 1964. 49. 41528
reverses wagons across the road through Staveley
Iron Works, 23rd May 1963. 50. Nos 32, 14 and 34;
three Hawthorn, Leslie 0-6-0 saddle tanks working
Corby Iron & Steel Works, 29th May 1966.

51. 65789, 63386 and 65828 in the shed yards at Blyth North, 11th June
1964. 52. 47280 approaches the Leek line with wagons from the
precincts of the closed North Staffordshire Railway Works,
Stoke-on-Trent as 48548 passes, giving assistance to eastbound coal
empties, 9th November 1964.

54

53. 48090 having its boiler re-filled in
Northampton shed, 30th April 1961. 54. *Sir
John,* an Avonside 0-6-0ST, at the NCB works,
Mountain Ash, 26th November 1969.

55. 48744 takes water at Buxton, 17th February 1968. 56. 48683 approaches Hartford East Junction with a Northwich – Wallerscote sidings freight, 18th July 1967. 57. 60527 *Sun Chariot* leaves Perth with an Aberdeen – Glasgow train, 18th June 1963.

SC 35385

LOAD 21 TONS DISTRIBUTED

58. 60034 *Lord Faringdon* heads the south-bound 'West Coast Postal' at Cumbernauld, 16th July 1964. 59. At 18.00hrs Hugh Dow prepares for the pick-up at Auchterarder, 17th July 1964. 60. 80015 leaves Clapham Junction with Post Office workers for Kensington Olympia, 18th August 1966. 61. 82019 crosses Chelsea railway bridge with a Kensington Olympia – Clapham Junction train, 6th April 1967.

62. 75077 on the approaches to Grosvenor Bridge and Victoria with a special train, 6th March
1967. 63. 44767 approaches Middleton Junction with a Manchester – York train, 14th July 1967.
64. 92038 propels its train past Helsby signal box to access the CLC, 21st July 1965.

65. 48619 leaves Leicester with a freight for Coalville, 17th October 1964. 66. No. 22, a R. Stephenson & Hawthorns 0-4-0ST, works Stella South Power Station, Blaydon, 22nd April 1967. 67. 63732 leaves Ollerton with coal for the west, 24th June 1963.

68

69

68. 6611 crosses Hawarden Bridge, Shotton with coal empties for Wrexham, 3rd April 1965. 69. 48723 with a Wrexham – Brymbo freight, banked by 75048, passes Southsea, 19th November 1966. 70. 48669 marshals a freight in Croes Newydd yards, Wrexham, 3rd December 1966. 71. Wrexham, Mold & Connah's Quay Railway.

73
74

72. 48424 at Dove Holes Dale with a stone train from Buxton, 17th February 1968. 73. 48720 leaves Northwich with a freight for Hartford, 9th February 1968. 74. De-icing at Hendon Junction, Sunderland, 15th January 1966.

75. 61055 at Shireoaks East with a westbound freight, 23rd February 1963.
76. 42618 at Woodend with a Worksop – Nottingham train,
23rd February 1963.

77. 90496 approaches Clowne with coal from Clipstone to the Sheffield area, 18th April 1964. 78. A Stanier Class 5 4-6-0 runs beside the Kent estuary between Grange-over-Sands and Arnside with a Barrow-Euston train, 12th January 1968.

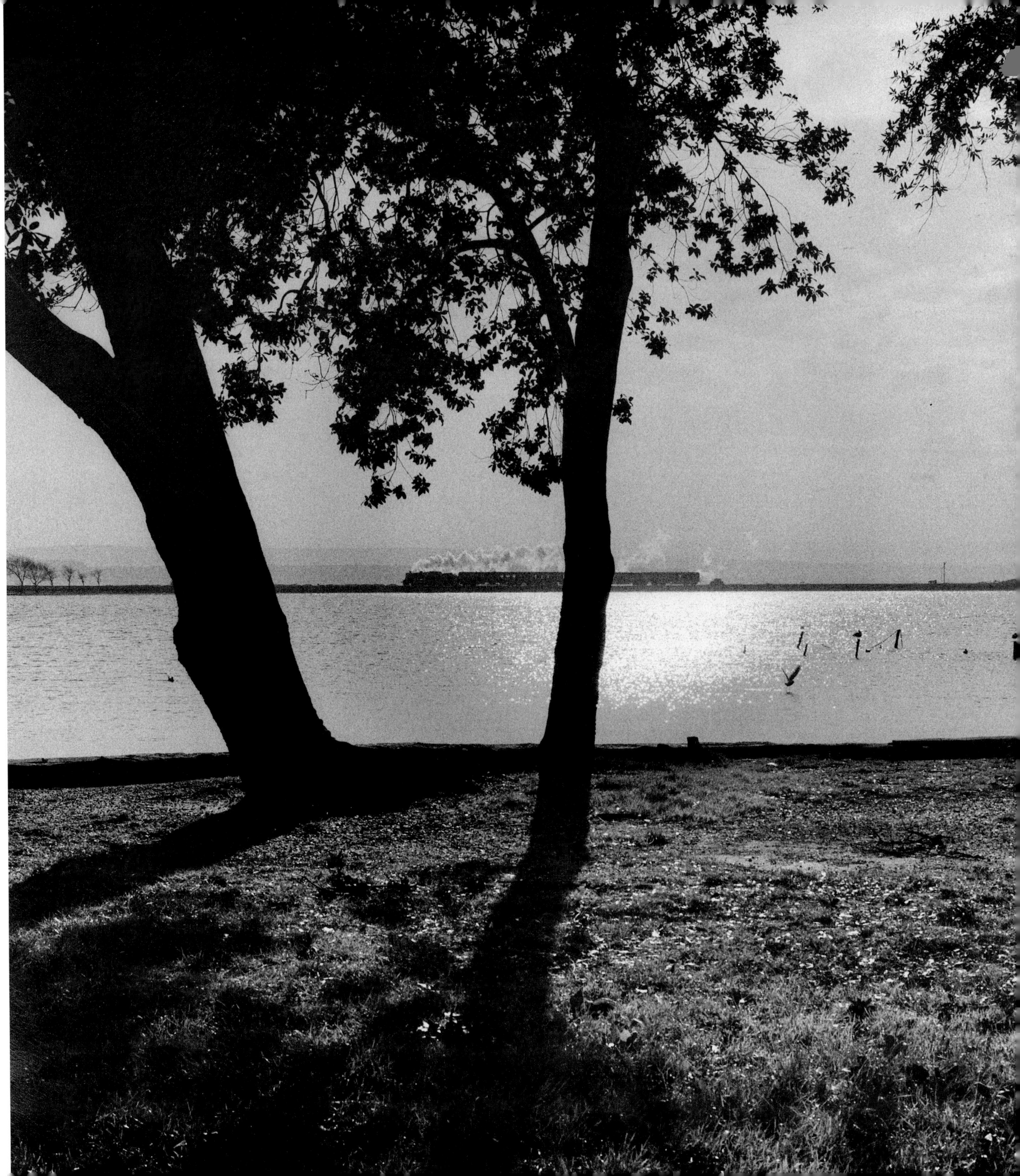

79. 76063 crosses Parkestone Bay, Poole with a Weymouth – Bournemouth train, 29th October 1966. 80. 32640 shortly after leaving Havant for Hayling Island, 9th December 1961. 81. 30313 runs along the shores of the Camel with a Padstow – Wadebridge train, 9th September 1959.

80
81

82

83

82. 4694 prepares to leave Wadebridge for Bodmin General as 30586 reverses past the motive power depot, 28th October 1961. 83. 4682 waits at Brecon with a Neath train as 46519 arrives from Moat Lane Junction, 7th September 1962. 84. 62566 arrives at Cambridge from Kings Lynn whilst 61091 waits to depart for King's Cross, 31st August 1958. 85. 80143 at Oxted with a Tunbridge Wells West train connects with 31278 on the all-stations push-pull to the same destination, 17th March 1962.

86. 30378 shortly after leaving Three Bridges
with the auto-train to East Grinstead,
7th October 1962. 87. 31521 with the
all-stations Oxted – Tunbridge Wells West
leaves Hurst Green, 17th March 1962.
88. 31544 near Worth with the Three Bridges –
East Grinstead push-pull, 7th October 1962.

89. 63976 approaches Whitwell Tunnel with southbound coal empties, 23rd October 1963. 90. 60139 *Sea Eagle* leaves New Southgate Tunnel with a King's Cross – Hull train, 1st June 1963. 91. 42981 between Dukinfield and Ashton with a northbound freight, 19th March 1966.

89
90

92. 48506 passes through Kearsley station with northbound empty stock, 23rd August 1967. 93. 45043 pulls into Warrington Bank Quay with a northbound passenger train and passes 45323 on a southbound freight, 6th August 1966. 94. A Manning, Wardle 0-6-0ST stands in Newdigate Streetchildren's playground in Aston, Birmingham, 24th September 1966.

92
93

95

95. 45565 *Victoria* at Crofton West Junction, 24th December 1964.
96. 90664 comes off Wakefield shed at Calder Bridge Junction,
24th December 1964.

97. 90122 passes Ryland's Sidings, north of Wigan with northbound coal empties banked by 90686,
11th November 1964. 98. 90130 approaches Worksop station with westbound empty coal wagons,
18th April 1964.

99. 90149 approaches Scunthorpe on Scotter Road Viaduct with an east-bound freight, 30th October 1965. 100. 90501 passes Trent Junction, Scunthorpe with a westbound steel train, 31st October 1965.

101. No.18, a Hunslet 0-6-0ST, shunts the yards of
Redbourn Iron & Steel Works, Scunthorpe, 31st October
1965. 102. A Class J27 0-6-0 shunts coal wagons at Blyth
North, 8th January 1966. 103. 48403 banks a freight out of
Stoke on the Derby line at Carters Crossing, 7th
November 1964.

104. 48767 reverses past Ryecroft Junction, Walsall on to the Sutton Coldfield line, 16th November 1963. 105. 65892 at Cambois, returning to Blyth North, 12th June 1964. 106. 48532 leaves Buxton and crosses Duke's Drive Viaduct en route to Hindlow, 3rd March 1967. 107. 48293 heads for Liverpool Docks at Walton, 20th November 1967.

104
105

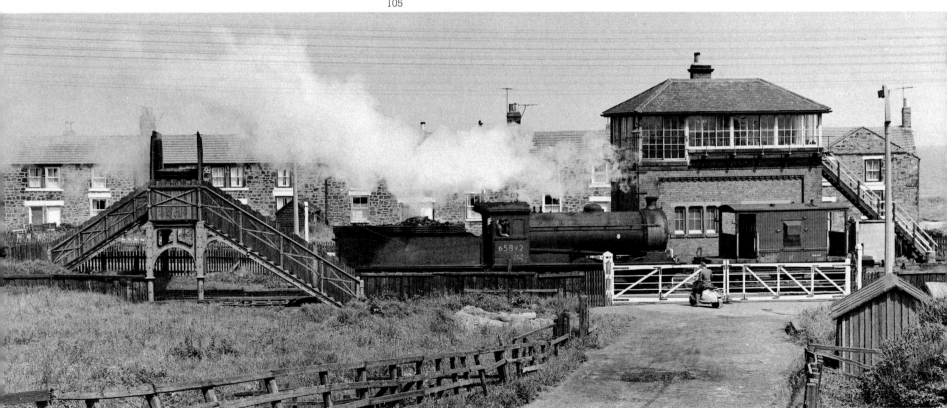

108. 45305 above Runcorn with a southbound freight, 22nd November 1967. 109. A Class 8F 2-8-0 approaches Runcorn station from Folly Lane, 22nd November 1967.

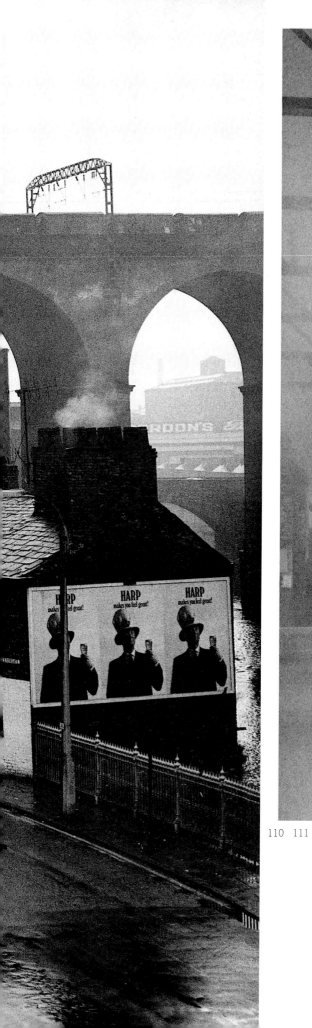

110. A Stanier Class 5 4-6-0 heads a southbound freight
over Stockport Viaduct, 3rd May 1968. 111. 70051
Firth of Forth at Crewe with a train for Barrow and
Windermere, 26th November 1966.

112/113. 44211 and 45608 *Gibraltar* at the west end of Birmingham New Street with parcel trains on 2nd August 1963 and 10th April 1964 respectively.

114. Rebuilding Leeds City station,
12th May 1963. 115. 90761 and 57665
in Motherwell shed, 6th July 1960.
116. 48057 crosses the River Mersey at
Warrington with a southbound
permanent way train, 6th August 1966.

114

117. 48682 crosses the Manchester Ship Canal south of Warrington with a northbound hopper train, 6th August 1966. 118. 3830 heads a westbound freight past the Severn Bridge near Lydney, 19th February 1965. 119. A Class Q6 0-8-0 crosses Seaton Viaduct over the River Wansbeck, with empty wagons for Ashington, 14th January 1966. 120. An Ebbw Vale train passes under Crumlin Viaduct, 25th March 1961.

121. An Amlwch – Bangor train stops at Llanfair',
4th September 1962. 122. A Derby – Nottingham
train leaves Basford and Bulwell, 15th August
1964. 123. A southbound parcels train runs
beneath Grayrigg Pike, south of Tebay,
29th November 1967.

123

124. 70011 *Hotspur* with a northbound mixed freight passes Harrison's Sidings, Shap, 30th November 1967. 125. 92058 takes the Crewe line at Chester with a mixed freight, 18th July 1967. 126. A Class A1 4-6-2 crosses the Royal Border Bridge, Berwick with a southbound cement train, 5th January 1962. 127. 1442 at Uffculme with a mixed milk and passenger train from Hemyock to Tiverton Junction, 27th April 1963.

124 125

128. 44978 waits in the spur at Helmsdale for passage
to follow the Wick and Thurso train to Inverness,
15th June 1962. 129. A Carmarthen – Aberystwyth
train waits at Pencader, 4th June 1964. 130. 60120
Kittiwake at Belle Isle with a King's Cross – Leeds train
passes 60157 *Great Eastern* light engine off
'Top Shed', 27th May 1963.

128

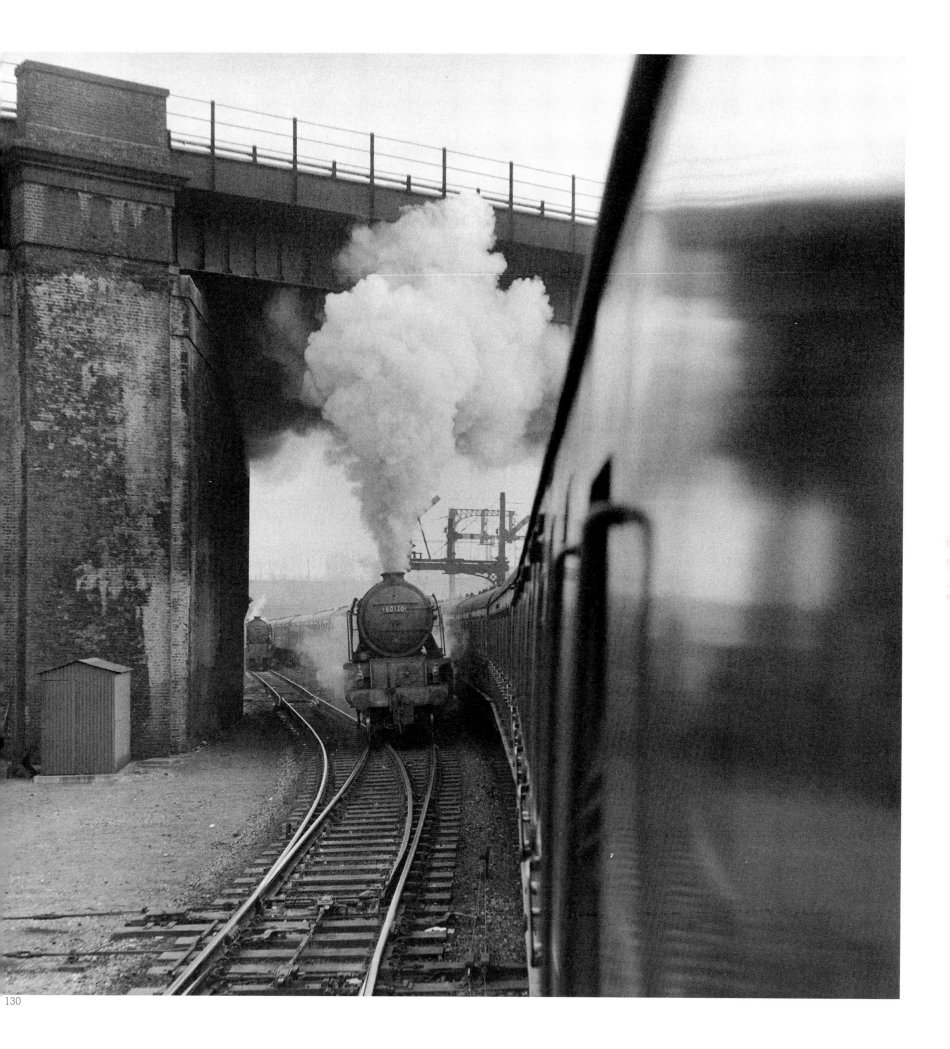

131

132

131. 60039 *Sandwich*, 60010 *Dominion of Canada*, 60033 *Seagull* and 60038 *Firdaussi* at King's Cross 'Top Shed', 4th October 1959. 132. 42149 under the coaling plant at Normanton with 90362 alongside, 12th May 1963. 133. 48005 on the turntable with 48201 behind, in Barrow Road roundhouse, Bristol, 14th February 1965.

134. 48613, 5910 *Park Hall*, 42814, 42958 and 42948 on Birkenhead shed, 23rd September 1961.
135. 92023 waits to proceed to Gowhole from the docks at Birkenhead, 21st August 1967.
136. 92023 at Blackpool Street Junction, Birkenhead with empty coal wagons, 22nd August 1967.

134
135

139

137. 45231 passes through derelict Spellow station, Liverpool with a freight from the docks, 19th April 1968. 138. 48409 with a freight leaves Swansea East Docks, 29th April 1961. 139. 65859 with freight for Middlesbrough Docks passes 65787 at Newport East Junction, 11th November 1961.

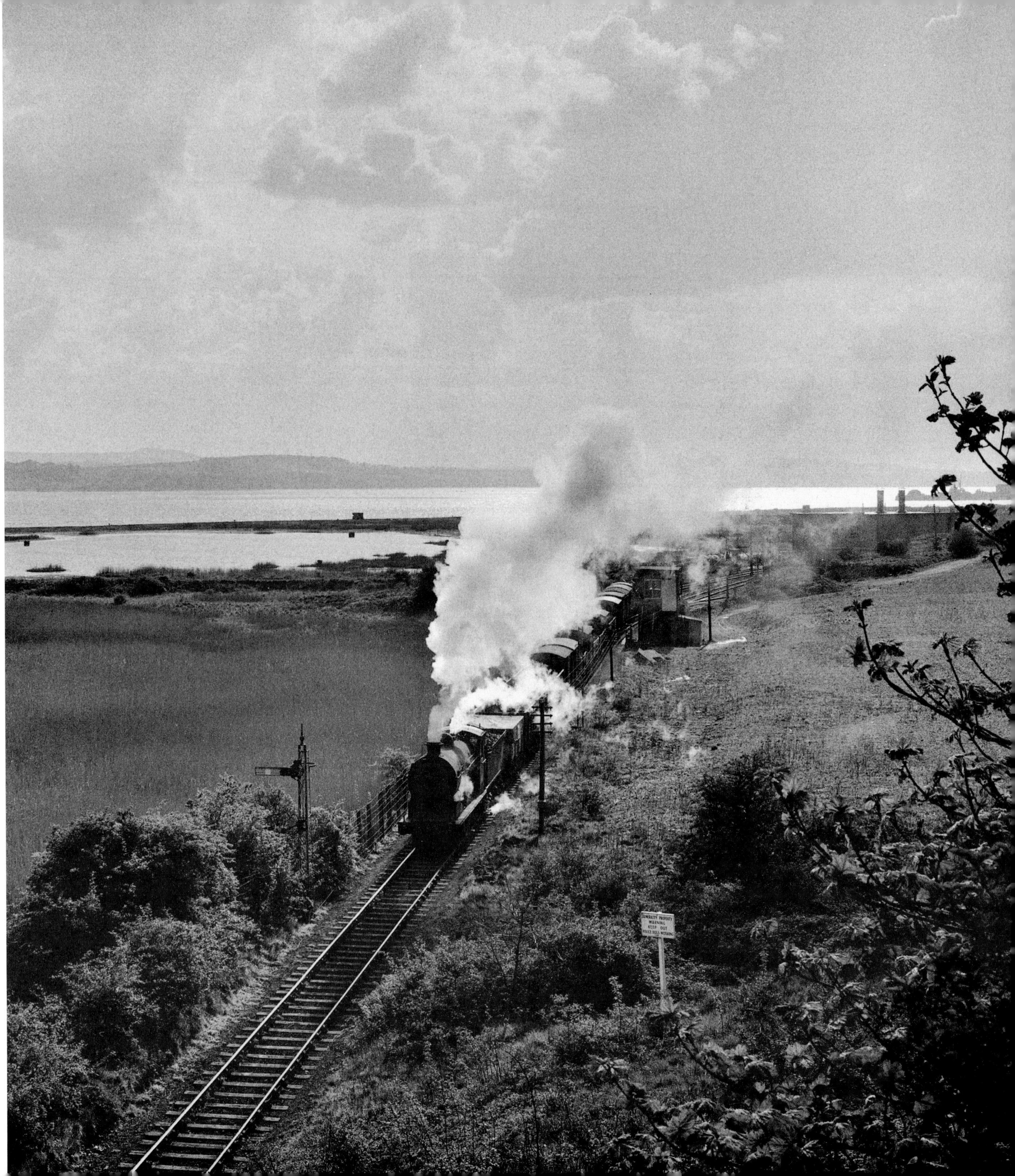
WARNING
KEEP OUT

140. 64623 leaves Rosyth Dockyard with freight for Inverkeithing, 12th May 1966.
141. 65858 south of Seghill with coal for the docks at Percy Main overhauls No. 41, a R. Stephenson & Hawthorns 0-4-0ST from Burradon Colliery, 19th November 1963.
142. 65663 passes Tyne Dock locomotive sheds with a freight from the docks, with 65864 light engine, 25th November 1961.

143. 48222 leaves Beverley Sidings, Goole for the docks, 2nd June 1967. 144. 82006 at Clapham Junction with a Kensington Olympia train, 28th July 1966. 145. No. 58, an Austerity type 0-6-0ST, at Derwenthaugh Coking Plant, 27th September 1969.

146. 84003 at Bala with the Bala Junction train, 5th June 1964. 147. 5399 leaves Barmouth for Wrexham and passes 75026. 148. 75026 follows with a Shrewsbury train, 4th September 1962.

149. No. 7 *Owain Glyndŵr* leaves Aberystwyth for Devil's Bridge, 4th June 1964.
150. 48668 approaches Stoke station with a northbound freight, 9th November 1964.
151. 41312 passes Corfe with a Swanage – Wareham train, 5th June 1965.

152. 45325 leaves Bangor with an extra train for Manchester, 19th April 1965. 153. 92182 passes Nottingham London Road, High Level station with a northbound coal train, 13th November 1965. 154. 45342 approaches Preston station with a southbound parcels train, 11th January 1968.

155. 65879 near Tunstall with a coal train from Silksworth to South Dock, Sunderland, 30th August 1967. 156. 45368 passes through Stalybridge with a northbound 'extra', 3rd June 1966. 157. 70006 *Robert Burns* with a train for Perth and 47326 with parcels vans at Carlisle, 10th June 1965.

158. 44910 at Liverpool Exchange with a
Glasgow train, 5th March 1967. 159. 73028
waits for the road with a train for Bristol at
Birmingham New Street, 11th April 1964.

160. 73109 brings a local train into Glasgow Queen Street passing 69188, station pilot, 20th July 1959. 161. 73145 south of Perth with a Dundee – Glasgow train, 5th July 1963. 162. 73072 arrives at Wemyss Bay with a train from Glasgow, 21st June 1963.

163. 73149 leaves Oban with a train for Glasgow, 4th July 1960.
164. 73011 with an eastbound train past Penmaenmawr, 23rd July 1965.
165. 73085 *Melisande* with a Bournemouth – Waterloo train leaves Brockenhurst, 5th November 1966.

166. 73135 passes Holbeck High, Leeds with
a southbound parcels train, 30th May 1967.
167. 45321 with a parcels train in Walsall
station, 21st December 1963.
168. 44683 at Blackburn with an eastbound
parcels train, 16th March 1968.

169. Waiting for a northbound train at Doncaster, 13th August 1965. 170. 42252 approaches Brighouse with a westbound parcels train, 20th May 1967. 171. 7815 *Fritwell Manor* at Carmarthen with a train for Aberystwyth, 4th June 1964. 172. 42084 near Hebden Bridge with a westbound parcels train, 9th June 1964.

173. 32347 shunts Crawley yards, 13th January 1962. 174. Accident in the Aldwych, 4th May 1963. 175. 70046 *Anzac* with a southbound parcels train south of Penrith, 1st March 1967.

173
174

176. 45056 at Burton-on-Trent with a southbound parcels train,
8th October 1961. 177. 90037 propels wagons across the River
Trent at Rectory Junction, east of Nottingham, 13th November 1965.

178

179

178. 30512 in the shed yard at Feltham with 34049 *Anti-Aircraft Command* on the turntable, 19th November 1960. 179. 35025 *Brocklebank Line*, 30831 and 30508 at Salisbury MPD, 23rd September 1962. 180. 31542, 31004 and 31065 in Dover shed, 19th March 1961. 181. 34002 *Salisbury* at Exmouth Junction shed, 29th October 1961.

182. 31837 near Egloskerry with the Padstow portion of the 'Atlantic Coast Express' for Waterloo, 9th September 1959. 183. 30850 *Lord Nelson* passes through Clapham Junction with a Bournemouth line train, 19th June 1959. 184. 30900 *Eton* with a Charing Cross – Hastings train passes 31878 and 31522 on Tonbridge shed, 28th May 1960.

185. 45459 and 46105 *Cameron Highlander* on Polmadie shed, Glasgow, 18th July 1961.
186. 45267, 45561 *Saskatchewan* and 46142 *The York & Lancaster Regiment* in Kentish Town roundhouse, 2nd August 1960.
187. 42723 and 42725 in Agecroft shed, 13th August 1961.

185

186

188. 46237 *City of Bristol* at Tring with the Glasgow – Euston 'Caledonian', 2nd April 1958. 189. 40655 and 45582 *Central Provinces* approach Kenton with an express from Euston, 4th April 1958. 190. 46201 *Princess Elizabeth* approaches Stirling with fish from Aberdeen, 20th July 1962.

188
189

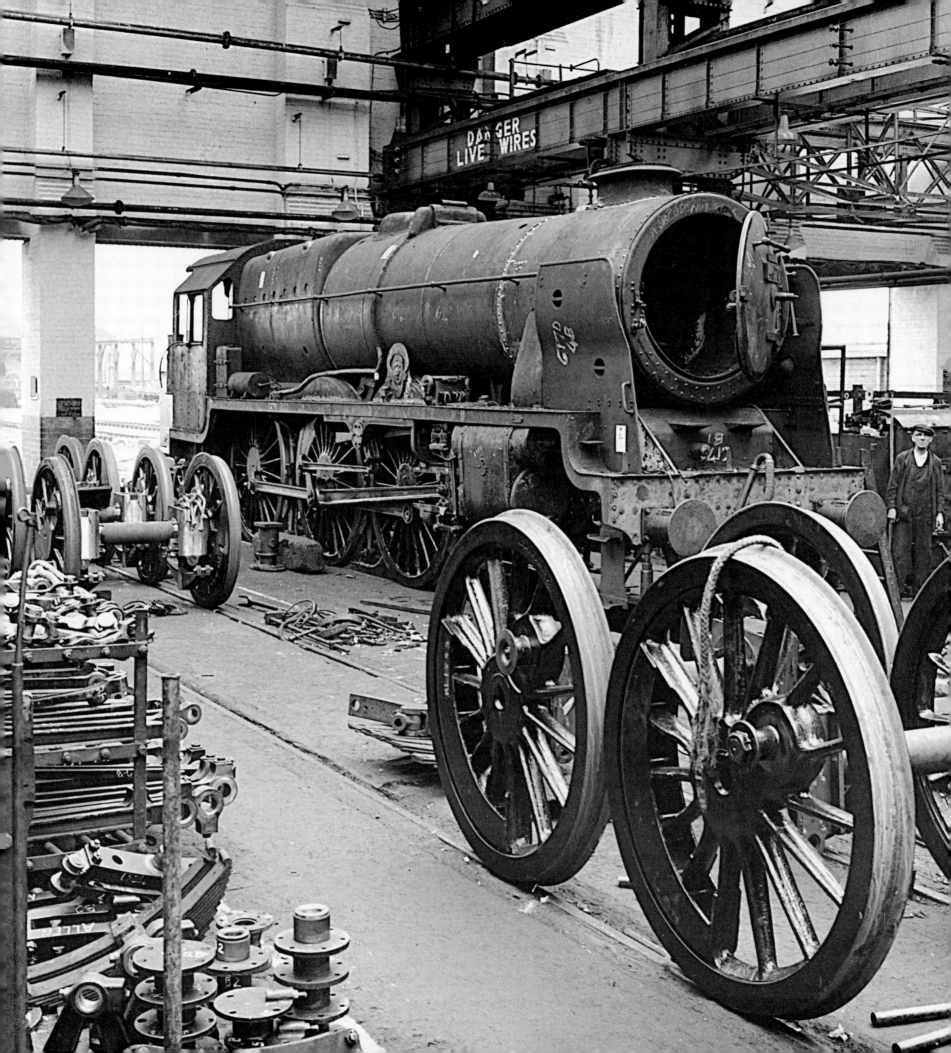

191. 46170 *British Legion* in Crewe Works,
20th August 1961. 192. 45175 (left) in St Rollox
Works, Glasgow, 21st June 1962. 193. 64628 in
Inverurie Works, 12th June 1962.

194. 60019 *Bittern* approaches Montrose with a train from Aberdeen to Glasgow, 6th May 1966. 195. 60520 *Owen Tudor* with a King's Cross – Edinburgh train north of Hatfield, 22nd December 1962. 196. 60828 with a train from Marylebone to Manchester near Saunderton, 27th May 1958.

197. 60052 *Prince Palatine* and 61354 in St Margarets locomotive shed, Edinburgh, 13th June 1965. 198. 65338, 64604, 64552 and 64617 in Dunfermline shed, 18th June 1962.

199. 5018 *St Mawes Castle* near Solihull with the Birmingham – Paddington 'Inter-City', 18th July 1958. 200. 6029 *King Edward VIII* passes through High Wycombe station with a Paddington – Birkenhead train, 6th May 1961. 201. 6808 *Beenham Grange* leaves Penzance shed, 28th October 1961.

202. 5927 *Guild Hall*, 7823 *Hook Norton Manor* and 4155 in Tyseley roundhouse.
203. 4155 (left) from the opposite side of the turntable with 5927, 6861 *Crynant Grange*, 5306 and 7823, 28th July 1963.

204. 6661 in Aberdare roundhouse, with 9607 behind, 9th March 1963. 205. 3843 with an eastbound coal train at Nelson and Llancaiach, 6th April 1963. 206. 5649 leaves Hengoed High Level with a Neath – Pontypool Road train, 19th May 1962.

204

BEWARE
OF THE
TRAINS

207. 6115 approaches Cefn-glas Tunnel as it leaves Quakers Yard High Level with a Pontypool Road – Neath train, 9th March 1963.
208. 65791 near Backworth with a coal train for Percy Main, 19th November 1963.
209. A pair of Class 8F 2-8-0s with a train of empty coal wagons at Fenton, Staffordshire, 28th November 1964.

207

208

210

211

210. 9600 works Merthyr
Vale Colliery, 3rd October
1968. 211. 92203 heads
away from Bidston with iron
ore for Shotton Steel Works,
25th February 1967.
212. 'Coal-pickers' at
Whitehaven, 10th June 1966.

213. NCB No. 18, a R. Stephenson & Hawthorns 0-6-0ST, works Blyth disposal point, 20th November 1963. 214. *Illtyd,* an Andrew Barclay 0-6-0ST, receives coal at Talywain, Abersychan, 8th May 1967. 215. 90016 passes Glasshaughton Colliery, Castleford with coal for Goole, 3rd June 1967.

216. 44920 leaves Ince Moss, Wigan with coal wagons for Leigh, 1st December 1967. 217. 42664 with southbound parcels vans leaves Wigan North Western yards and approaches 48338 on the main line, 12th November 1964.

218. 75015 shunts the yards at Wigan Wallgate, 12th November 1964.
219. 45073 passes through Nelson with a Colne – Preston parcels train,
11th July 1968.

221

220. 42422 with a school train for Great Malvern crosses the Worcester
& Birmingham Canal between Shrub Hill and Foregate Street stations,
Worcester, 27th July 1961. 221. 63395 approaches Ryhope from South Dock,
Sunderland, with coal empties for South Hetton, 31st August 1967.

222. A Class 8F 2-8-0 near Cromford with an eastbound freight, 31st May 1966. 223. 68012 at
Longcliffe with tenders for Middleton Top, 3rd March 1967. 224. 47000 returns to Sheep Pasture from
Middleton Quarry at Bolehill, 1st June 1966.

225. The water tank at Middleton Top,
1st June 1966. 226 61324 passes under the
pseudo-Doric arch supporting the water tanks
at Inverness locomotive shed, 22nd July 1959.
227. 63647 with eastbound coal empties passes
48215 watering at Worksop West,
23rd February 1963.

225
226

228. 48100 leaves Frodingham in the direction of Doncaster with two withdrawn Class O4 2-8-0s, 31st October 1965. 229. 56298 and 56359 (pair), 57418, 57319, 57463, 55201, 57369, 55267, 57288, 57417 and 56313 (centre row) with 57325, 57593, 57271, 57564, 57389, 57268 and 57563 (back row) withdrawn at Carnbroe, Coatbridge, 20th June 1962. 230. 45668 *Madden* passes the scrap yard at Tapton Junction, Chesterfield, with a train from Gloucester to Sheffield, 23rd May 1963. 231. 55232 and 40614 being cut up at Inverurie, 12th June 1962.

232. 65789 enters North Blyth roundhouse, 11th June 1964. 233. 48687 beside Brinnington Junction, signal box, Stockport, 4th May 1968. 234. Permanent way gang at the east end of Edinburgh Waverley, 18th June 1964.

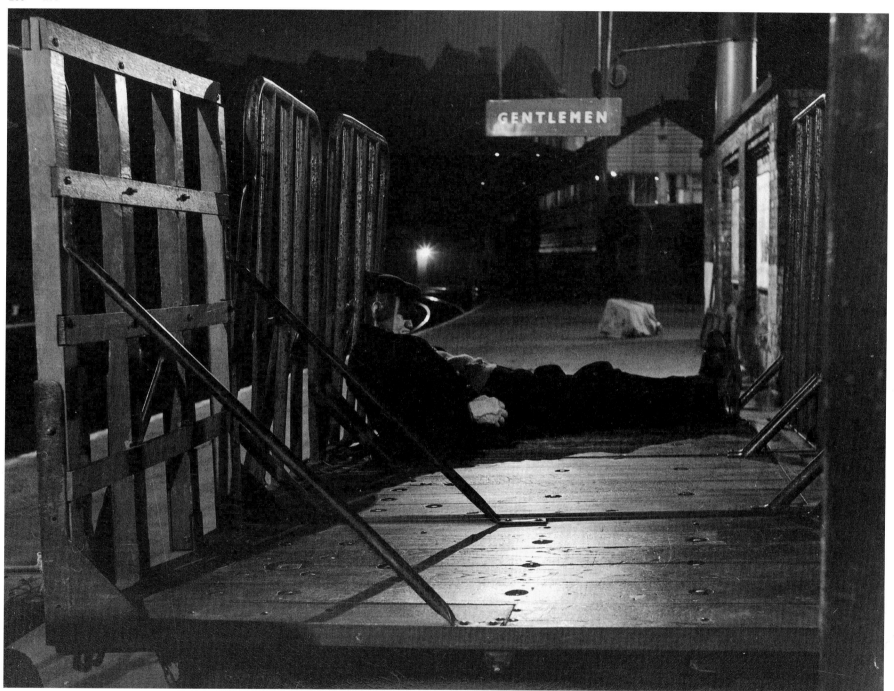

235. Wigan Central. 236. Birmingham New Street.

237/8/9. Commemorating the end of British Railways steam: 70013 *Oliver Cromwell* passes over Batty Moss Viaduct, Ribblehead and on to Blea Moor Tunnel with the 'Fifteen Guinea Special' from Liverpool to Carlisle, 11th August 1968.

MVS